Brands We Know

Minecraft

By Sara Green

Bellwether Media • Minneapolis, MN.

Jump into the cockpit and take flight with Pilot books. Your journey will take you on high-energy adventures as you learn about all that is wild, weird, fascinating, and fun!

This edition first published in 2017 by Bellwether Media, Inc.

Library of Congress Cataloging-in-Publication Data

Names: Green, Sara, 1964- author.
Title: Minecraft / by Sara Green.
Description: Minneapolis, MN : Bellwether Media, Inc., 2017. | Series: Pilot: Brands
We Know | Includes bibliographical references and index.
Identifiers: LCCN 2016001371 | ISBN 9781626174108 (hardcover : alk. paper)
ISBN 9781618912695 (paperback : alk. paper)
Subjects: LCSH: Minecraft (Game)--Juvenile literature.
Classification: LCC GV1469.35.M535 G74 2017 | DDC 794.8--dc23
LC record available at http://lccn.loc.gov/2016001371

Printed in the United States of America, North Mankato, MN.

MINECRAFT

Table of Contents

What Is Minecraft?

Millions of people build and explore in the world of *Minecraft*. In this game, players collect **resources** and **craft** items. They place blocks to create castles, rockets, railroads, or whatever their minds can imagine!

Minecraft is a 3D **sandbox video game** developed by a company called Mojang. The company **headquarters** is in Stockholm, Sweden. *Minecraft* can be single or multi-player. The game can be played on computers, **consoles**, and mobile devices.

Minecraft has won many awards. In 2011, it won Best Downloadable Game and the **Innovation** Award from the Game Developers Choice Awards. Four years later, it won the Kids' Choice Award for Most Addicting Game! *Minecraft* has also expanded into other areas. People can buy *Minecraft* toys, t-shirts, and other items. The game also helps students learn in the classroom. With so much to offer, *Minecraft* continues to attract new fans. Today, it is one of the most popular video game **brands** on Earth!

more than
100 million
users in 2014

more than
70 million
total games sold

more than
22 million
computer games sold

more than
50
Mojang
employees

more than
30
types of mobs

5

The Journey Begins

A Swedish man named Markus "Notch" Persson created *Minecraft*. As a young man, Notch enjoyed playing video games. He especially liked the type that allowed him to build things. He decided to make a similar game of his own. In his computer game, players mined ore. They also crafted things from a variety of resources. These tasks inspired Notch to name his game *Minecraft*.

Busy Builder
In less than a week, Notch created the first version of *Minecraft*. He based the game off of *Infiniminer*, another sandbox digging game that uses blocks.

Markus "Notch" Persson

Notch released the first version of *Minecraft* to the public in 2009. It became popular right away! Notch could not improve the game by himself. Soon, he helped start a video game company called Mojang. Notch and Mojang's developers made the *Minecraft* world bigger. People loved it even more. *Minecraft* was on its way to becoming one of the most successful video games of all time.

Let's Play!

Minecraft is built from a person's imagination. It does not have a story or rules like most other video games. Users control a main character called the Player. The game is usually in **first-person point of view**. Whoever is playing sees what the Player sees. Throughout the game, other online users can show up. Sometimes **mobs** appear. Some mobs are friendly, such as farm animals and villagers. Others, such as creepers and skeletons, are **hostile**.

the Overworld

The game begins somewhere in the Overworld. Here, players can explore more than ten main types of **biomes**. These include grasslands, swamps, and forests. Players must build a special **portal** to get to another area called the Nether. This area is filled with dangers, such as fire, lava, and scary creatures. The Nether is also very dark. Players can get lost easily. The final area is called the End. It is a large island floating in the sky. Players can battle the Ender Dragon there.

Watch the Time!

The game cycles between day and night. Daytime is safer. Players can explore, gather resources, and craft tools. Nighttime is more dangerous. Players often find shelter from deadly mob attacks.

skeleton

Minecraft allows players to choose how they want to play. People who only want to build and explore can select creative **mode**. Resources are easily available. Players remain safe from enemies and other dangers. People who want more challenges can choose survival mode. Players must find resources and food. They face monsters, injuries, and other threats. However, if players die, they can come back to life and return to the same game. Players can also choose hardcore mode. When players die, they must create a new game.

In adventure mode, players cannot destroy or add blocks unless they have the correct tools. This means that they must navigate the world as it is. In **spectator** mode, players are invisible! They fly through the *Minecraft* world without fear. They can even see the world through the eyes of mobs.

This adventure is up to you

2010s tagline

Not Always Bad

When hostile mobs are killed, they may drop items. String from spiders is used for bows or fishing poles. Spider eyes can be used for potions.

Hostile Mobs

Name	Weapon	Drops
blaze	fireballs	blaze rod
cave spider	poison	spider eye, string
creeper	explosives	gunpowder
guardian	laser beam, thorns	crystals, fish
silverfish	none	none
skeleton	arrows	armor, arrows, bones, bow
slime	none	slime balls
witch	potions	potion ingredients
wither	skulls	nether star
zombie	none	rotten flesh

witch

zombie

blaze

Releases and Changes

Minecraft was originally created for computers. However, it soon expanded. In 2011, *Minecraft: Pocket Edition* was released. Now people could play *Minecraft* on their smartphones and other mobile devices. *Minecraft* is also available for consoles. *Minecraft* for Xbox 360 came on the market in 2012. It sold more than one million copies in its first week! Versions for Xbox One, PlayStation 3, and PlayStation 4 soon followed. In 2015, *Minecraft* was released for Wii U.

Build! Craft! Explore!

2010s *Minecraft* for PS3 tagline

Xbox 360

Over time, Mojang headquarters also saw changes. In 2011, Notch stepped down from his role as the game's lead designer. A developer named Jens "Jeb" Bergensten took his place. Then in 2014, a company called Microsoft bought Mojang for $2.5 billion. Notch left the company to seek other interests. However, exploring the *Minecraft* world is still as exciting as ever. The current developers continue to add new surprises. Who knows what the future holds!

Jens Bergensten

Wolf Whisperer

Jens Bergensten helped create wolves in the game. Players can tame wild wolves with bones. Then, the wolves can sit and stay on command!

More Than a Game

Minecraft fans enjoy the game in other ways. Most years, Mojang hosts an event called Minecon. Fans gather and meet their online friends. Competitions test players' abilities to finish games in the fastest times. **Panels** and other events showcase the latest *Minecraft* products. Some people even dress up as their favorite creatures! Minecon received the Guinness World Record for "Largest Convention for a Single Video Game" in 2015.

People can enjoy *Minecraft* in other ways. In 2014, fans were excited to hear that a movie is being planned. In 2015, Mojang and Telltale Games released a separate video game called *Minecraft: Story Mode*. Unlike *Minecraft*, the story mode game has a beginning and an end. Players make decisions that affect the game's story.

A Green Monster
The creeper was supposed to be a pig. Notch accidentally made the character tall and narrow instead of short and fat.

Minecon costume

MINECON
ORLANDO, FL 2013

The brand has a lot of **merchandise**. People can buy plush creepers and foam swords. *Minecraft* clothing and jewelry are available. People can also play with *Minecraft* LEGO sets. They can hide from a skeleton in The Farm or fight a creeper in The Mine!

Minecraft can help children learn in several ways. Some programs teach users how to write computer code. One is the **software** LearnToMod, that is added to *Minecraft*. It shows players how to do tricks, such as building doors that block zombies.

Teachers began using *MinecraftEdu* in their classrooms in 2011. Students in more than 40 countries use *MinecraftEdu* for many subjects, including science, history, and **architecture**.

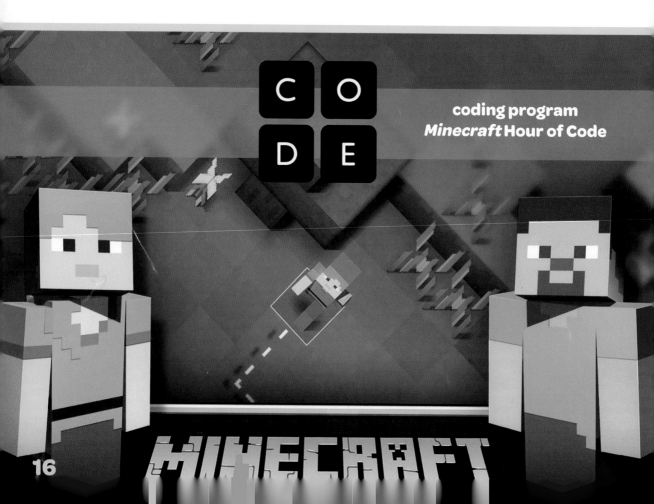

coding program
Minecraft **Hour of Code**

In 2016, Microsoft announced an updated version called *Minecraft: Education Edition*. New features include student login and the ability to save work. In the latest edition, students can explore ancient temples or visit the South Pole. Some may even view the inside of an eyeball!

. . . .

Classroom Adventures

In 2013, a school in Stockholm, Sweden, made *Minecraft* a requirement for its 13-year-old students!

Block by Block

Minecraft helps the world in another way. A **United Nations** project called Block by Block uses *Minecraft* to improve areas around the world. First, Block by Block recreates communities in the game. Then, community members take over and can add fun features like parks and playgrounds. They can also make online visits to see what ideas are in place and make changes if they want. When the model is finished, architects and builders start making the real-life structure.

One Block by Block project improved a sports field in Nairobi, Kenya. Another helped farmers in Haiti design a sea wall to prevent flooding. They also added public bathrooms to the area. With *Minecraft*, people can build anything they can imagine!

. . . .

Protecting Wildlife

Animal protection group United for Wildlife uses *Minecraft* for their cause. Their map, **We are the Rangers**, teaches about illegal hunting. In it, players rescue and protect animals.

We are the Rangers map

Minecraft Timeline

2011
Jens "Jeb" Bergensten becomes lead *Minecraft* developer in November

2009
Markus "Notch" Persson releases an early version of *Minecraft* to the public

2010
MinecraftCon, now called Minecon, is first held in Bellevue, Washington

2012
Minecraft for the Xbox 360 is available

MOJANG

2009
Mojang is founded

2011
Minecraft: Pocket Edition is launched in August

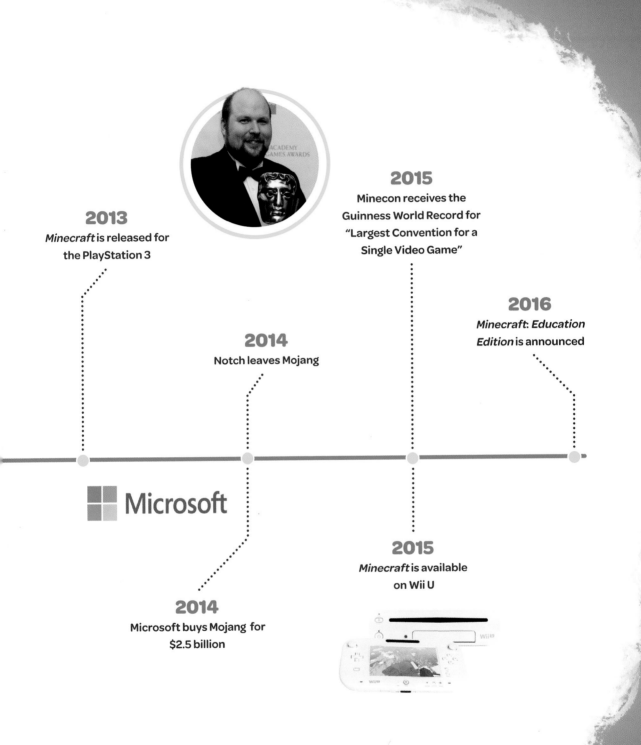

2013
Minecraft is released for
the PlayStation 3

2015
Minecon receives the
Guinness World Record for
"Largest Convention for a
Single Video Game"

2016
*Minecraft: Education
Edition* is announced

2014
Notch leaves Mojang

Microsoft

2015
Minecraft is available
on Wii U

2014
Microsoft buys Mojang for
$2.5 billion

Glossary

architecture—the art of designing buildings and other structures

biomes—nature communities defined by their climate, land features, and living things

brands—categories of products all made by the same company

consoles—electronic devices for playing video games on a television screen

craft—to build or create

first-person point of view—an angle in which a player views the action through the eyes of the character he or she is controlling

headquarters—a company's main office

hostile—not friendly

innovation—a new method, product, or idea

merchandise—items sold in a store

mobs—creatures that appear and move around in *Minecraft*

mode—a way of playing *Minecraft*

panels—groups of people who answer questions in front of an audience

portal—an important doorway

resources—supplies that are collected and used as needed

sandbox video game—a type of video game that is usually open-ended; sandbox video games often include tools that allow the player to change the game world.

software—a program that tells a computer what to do

spectator—a person who watches a show, game, or event

United Nations—an international organization formed to promote peace

To Learn More

AT THE LIBRARY

Green, Sara. *Nintendo*. Minneapolis, Minn.: Bellwether Media, 2016.

Zeiger, James. *Minecraft Beginner's Guide*. Ann Arbor, Mich.: Cherry Lake Publishing, 2016.

Zeiger, James. *Minecraft: Mining and Farming*. Ann Arbor, Mich.: Cherry Lake Publishing, 2016.

ON THE WEB

Learning more about Minecraft is as easy as 1, 2, 3.

1. Go to www.factsurfer.com.

2. Enter "Minecraft" into the search box.

3. Click the "Surf" button and you will see a list of related web sites.

With factsurfer.com, finding more information is just a click away.

Index